Beginner's Guitar Lessons: The Es

Published by **www.fundamental-changes.co**

ISBN: 978-1483930459

www.fundamental-changes.com

Also by Joseph Alexander

The CAGED System and 100 Licks for Blues Guitar

The Complete Guide to Playing Blues Guitar Book One: Rhythm Guitar

The Complete Guide to Playing Blues Guitar Book Two: Melodic Phrasing

The Complete Guide to Playing Blues Guitar Book Three: Beyond Pentatonics

The Complete Guide to Playing Blues Guitar Compilation

Complete Technique for Modern Guitar

The Complete Technique, Theory and Scales Compilation for Guitar

Fundamental Changes in Jazz Guitar I: The Major ii V I for Bebop Guitar

Minor ii V Mastery for Jazz Guitar

Jazz Blues Soloing for Guitar

Guitar Scales in Context

Guitar Chords in Context Part One

Jazz Guitar Chord Mastery (Guitar Chords in Context Part Two)

Sight Reading Mastery for Guitar

Rock Guitar Un-CAGED: The CAGED System and 100 Licks for Rock Guitar

The Practical Guide to Modern Music Theory for Guitarists

All the Audio Examples in this book are available for *free* download from
www.fundamental-changes.com/audio-downloads

Contents

Introduction

I've written a lot of books on guitar, but I've never really felt it appropriate to write a beginner's book until now. There are so many products on the market which claim to make you play guitar like a God in a couple of weeks… How can I compete with that?

I've been teaching guitar for sixteen years now. Music has taken me all around the world: I have about fourty weekly students, and I love my job. I feel like I'm a success at what I do, and I enjoy sharing music with people of all ages. Over time, I have developed a bit of a system, which forms the basis of about the first fifteen lessons I teach. I don't stick to it rigidly because every new student has different needs, but if I can use it, I find that it produces *extremely* quick results.

I think it's fair to say that even if the student has even the smallest amount of aptitude at guitar, they'll go from nothing to being able to strum out a couple of tunes in less than ten lessons.

A good point to make here is that most people (*always* adults) tell me in their first lesson that they're 'tone deaf', or have 'no rhythm'. I have NEVER found someone I can't teach. Some may be (much) more challenging than others but there is always a way, I promise you.

I tell you this not to brag in my sparkly new book, but just to let you know that if you get the right teacher, you *will* be able to play the guitar.

Tone deaf people, in my experience, do not exist. If you can hear the difference between a firework exploding and a whistle blowing, you are not tone deaf. While distinguishing between tones is a skill that may take some refining, if you can hear that one noise is low and boomy, and another is a screechy whine, you can hear notes well enough to improve.

As for rhythm, if you can walk without falling over or going round in a circle, then you have enough rhythm to strum through a tune. End of story.

For a beginner, playing the guitar is about muscle memory, nothing more. Your strumming hand goes up and down in time and your *fretting* hand (chords/notes, etc.) moves between positions on the guitar neck. Piece them together and you're there. If you're an adult reading this and you can drive, you're already doing something much more complicated than playing the guitar. (The guitar also has the added advantage that if you lose concentration, you're unlikely to wrap it around a tree.)

If you don't drive, think about how you learned to walk. Obviously you don't remember that, but the process is the same. You're sending a signal from your brain to your muscles trying to get them to fire in the correct order, training them to be in the right place at the right time, and gradually making them stronger and more under your control.

My number one piece of advice is to get a good teacher. Don't learn online at first, it's an easy market for teachers to teach via Skype and YouTube these days, and can both be helpful after a while, but you need a teacher to give you feedback on your posture, hand position and all sorts of little things.
I'm forever moving my students' hands and fingers in the first couple of lessons. Holding a plectrum is particularly 'weird' at first. You need someone to nag you!

Also, have a goal in mind. There is nothing worse for a teacher than the student who 'just wants to play guitar' and when pressed on the matter say they 'like everything' or 'Dunno really.' I teach almost everything, but I won't force a student into what I like to play. I play jazz mostly… I'd lose a lot of students if I made them do that. (Don't worry; there's nothing remotely *jazzy* in this book!) Pick a song or a style. Working towards a goal will get you somewhere **much** faster than meandering aimlessly around the guitar, your teacher will like you, and you'll have a lot more fun with a greater sense of achievement.

This book isn't going to get you to professional levels. (In fact no book will, despite what they promise you.) This is an extremely concise, to-the-point set of fifteen lessons that show you a fantastic system to learn your chords and basic rhythm. I do not promise anything more than that.

The onus is on you. **You need to practice.** Ideally fifteen minutes twice a day. If your fingers get sore, and they will, *put the guitar down!* Take a break. Practice in the way I teach you in each lesson and you will make progress.

Do not practice for more than 15 minutes at any one time. Stick to the **exercises** while you're **practicing** but play whatever you like when you're **playing**. Practicing and playing are very different things.

Good Luck!

P.S. A common misconception that I hear ALL the time is that you should learn on an acoustic guitar and then 'graduate' to an electric. That's a load of rubbish. It's much easier to learn on an electric and transfer those skills to the acoustic guitar later.

All the Audio Examples in this book are available for *free* download from

www.fundamental-changes.com/audio-downloads

Lesson 1: Important Things You Should Know

The most important, and most often forgotten thing that I teach my students in the very first lesson is that the **guitar should balance.** This is the same whether you're playing an acoustic or electric guitar.

Electric Guitars have a natural advantage over acoustic guitars in that they are designed to balance on your *right* knee. Look at **photo 1a:**

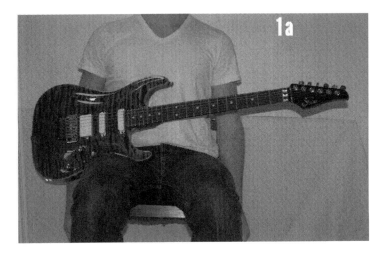

You will see me balancing the guitar on my knee and not touching it with my arms. This feels a bit unstable at first, like it's going to fall over, but it won't. As you lower your strumming arm onto the guitar it will give some extra support, but the most important thing is that you are not taking *any* of the weight of the guitar in the fretting (normally the left) hand. If you are taking any of the weight with your fretting hand, then you are restricting the range of movement possible on the frets.

Acoustic Guitars operate on the same principle; however, they do not naturally balance. You need to support the weight of the guitar by placing your bicep on the top of the guitar body as in **photo 1b.**

Again, if you were to remove your fretting hand from the guitar, the instrument shouldn't really move at all. **The guitar should still be on your *right* knee.**

If you're right handed like me, then you will use your left hand to play chords and melodies on the neck of the guitar. To communicate, we use the following simple system to number the fingers on the left hand.

Your index finger is 'finger 1', your middle finger is 2, ring, 3 and pinkie, 4. It's not rocket science, but it is really important to use the correct fingers for each chord when you're learning. This has far reaching consequences when you start to play more intricate things, but just trust me for now.

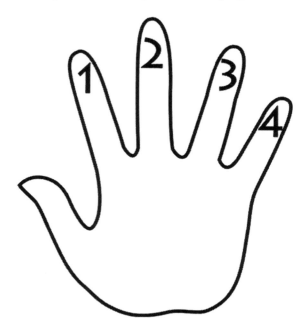

It is important at all times to play on the tips of your fingers. This is tricky at first, and they will get sore. When they start to hurt, take a break.

Compare **photos 1c** and **1d**. **Photo 1c** shows the correct finger position on the tips and **photo 1d** shows incorrect positioning; notice how the fingers are flat and brushing against adjacent strings.

Keep the nails of your fretting hand very short. I appreciate this isn't ideal if you're a lady, but there really is no way around it. If your nails stick out beyond the end of your fingers, there is no way to make a good contact between your fingers, the string, and the fretboard.

Finally, place your fingers *just behind the metal fret wire*. Remember twanging a ruler on the desk as school? If there is a lot of guitar string between your finger and the fret, like in **photo 1e,** then the string acts as that ruler. The correct position is shown in **photo 1f.** It isn't always possible to keep your fingers right against the frets, but you should make an effort to place them as close as possible to them.

That's enough 'rules', let's play!

Lesson 2: First Chords and Changes

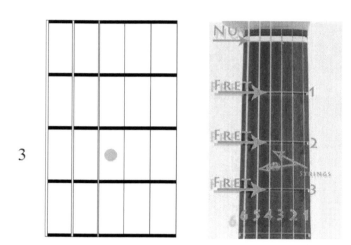

Look at the diagrams above. They show a similar section of the guitar neck.

The thick line at the top of the first picture is the *nut* of the guitar. You can think of this as *zero* on the guitar. The vertical lines are *strings,* which we press against the horizontal *frets*. As we press the string against successive frets, the string gets shorter, and this changes the note. The first fret is referred to as *fret 1;* the next highest (moving towards you) is *fret 2,* and then *fret 3,* etc.

The strings are slightly trickier to name. From left to right they are numbered 6, 5, 4, 3, 2 and then 1. The 6th string is the *bass* string and string 1 is the *highest* string.

Now check out the *map* below in **Audio Example 2a:**

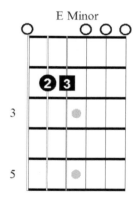

Essentially, wherever I have put a red dot, you put a finger. Be careful *which* fingers you use though; as the diagram shows that you use your 2nd and 3rd fingers.

The *hollow* dots above the strings show which strings you strum. In this case there is a hollow dot on each string without a fretted note already marked, so you strum *every* string in this chord.

The square dots are the roots or 'bass notes' of the chord; for example, the note, 'E' in the chord of E minor. The circular dots are the other notes that go to make up the chord. This isn't important for now, just concentrate on where the dots are and which fingers to use!

You should now have your 2nd and 3rd fingers just behind the 2nd fret on the 5th and 4th strings, as far on the tips as possible. The pad of your thumb should be on the back of the guitar neck and pointing towards the ceiling as shown in **photo 2a**:

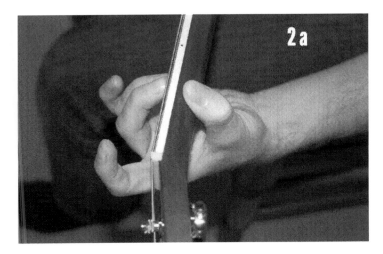

Strum softly and firmly down through all six strings.

Don't worry if the sound is a bit buzzy at first; see if you can adjust your hand position to eliminate any fret buzz.

The trick to learning the guitar at this stage is simply a case of repetition. It isn't exciting, cool or sexy, but you do need to train your fingers to hit the same spot each time. If you imagine the number of times David Beckham hit *that* free kick or Roger Federer practiced his serve, you get the idea. Playing the guitar is easier, but we still need to build muscle memory.

I would like you to now to place and remove your 2nd and 3rd fingers on that exact same E minor chord 10 times. Don't even bother to strum it; just make sure you can bring your two fingers down in the same place each time.

When you can do that, strum the chord each time you place it down.

Congratulations, you can now play your first chord on the guitar.

Look at the following chord of A minor: in particular look at the 4th and 3rd strings. Notice that the two fingers from E minor have moved across (or down) a string, and you have simply added your first finger to the 2nd string, 1st fret. You can hear this in **Audio Example 2b:**

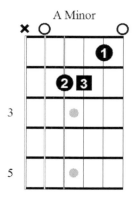

A Minor

To play the chord of A minor, start with E minor and slide your fingers one string down towards the floor. Then add your 1st finger on the second string. Try it and give it a strum. Remember to keep your thumb pointing towards the ceiling with just the pad of the thumb on the neck.

Repeat the process of removing and replacing your fingers ten times without strumming. When you can place your fingers down confidently add in a downward strum, but this time omit the 6th (bass) string. Look at the diagram again and notice the 'x' on the 6th string. This means don't strum it.

Let's start making some music. The notation below shows one way in which musicians communicate. Study **Audio Example 2c:**

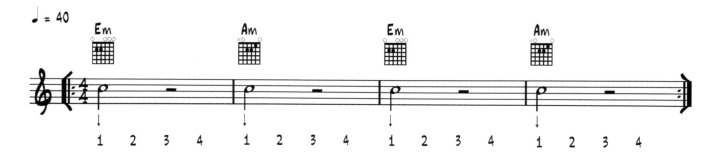

The first bar shows the chord of E minor. You are going to strum the chord on beat one. As soon as you have strummed it, use the three remaining beats to move to A minor.

Always strum in the direction shown by the arrow.

At this stage, do not worry about letting each chord ring for the full four beats. The objective is to be ready with the next chord before the '1' of the following bar. In other words, forget the sound and concentrate on staying in rhythm.

Metronomes are an extremely important tool throughout your development as a musician and extremely helpful as a beginner. If you have a smartphone, there are plenty of free metronomes to download so there is no excuse for not having one. In my experience, *students who practice with a metronome improve significantly faster than the ones who don't bother.*

In the above example, the metronome mark says play at 40 *beats per minute.* Set your metronome to 40 'bpm' and count 4 clicks for each bar.

Don't worry about buzzes, or holding down the chord for the full length of each bar. Just make sure you're ready for the new chord on beat one.

Now you have understood the basics, the following chapters are less 'wordy' and more hands-on.

All the Audio Examples in this book are available for *free* download from
www.fundamental-changes.com/audio-downloads

Lesson 3: Holding the Plectrum (Pick)

Plectrums are quite tricky to get used to at first and one of the most common problems to correct with new students, especially adults who have been playing a while.

Firstly, the quality of your plectrum is *very* important. If you go to see a national concert orchestra, the lead violinist is often playing a violin worth in excess of $1 million. The bow, just the stick and horse hair they use, can be upwards of $40,000. We use a $0.40c piece of plastic. In the tonal stakes we have a lot of catching up to do.

Remember, the plectrum determines the tone of *every* note that the guitar produces. If your pick is too thin, you get too much 'clack' as it moves across the strings.

While choice of pick is a personal choice, make sure to start with one that is over 1mm thick. I recommend **Jim Dunlop 1.5mm picks** to all my students. They're well-made and produce excellent tone.

You should hold the plectrum between *the pad of the thumb and the <u>side</u> of the index finger.* I can't stress this enough!

Look at **photo 3a:**

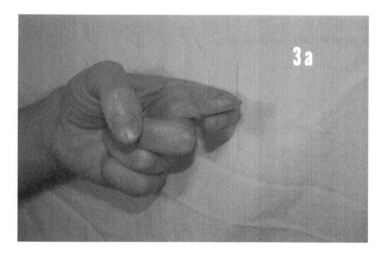

Notice that the pick balances nicely on the edge of my finger. It is **not** on the pad. The thumb *pad* then comes across and sits on top of the plectrum so that only 2-3mm or 1/8th of an inch sticks out as shown in **photo 3b:**

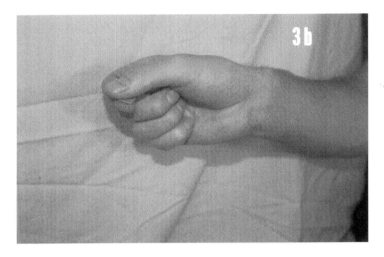

If you get this part right, when you move your hand to the guitar strings, the pick should lie fairly parallel to the strings. Rest the pick against the strings as shown in **photo 3c:**

Finally, we want to hold the plectrum at a slight angle so it glides through the strings when you strum. To achieve this, *pinch* your index finger and thumb together very slightly to make an angle of about 30° between the pick and the string. This is shown in **photo 3d:**

Now the pick will slide through each string with a minimum of resistance in whichever direction you strum.

My biggest piece of advice is not to over grip the plectrum. It should be light and bobble around a bit when you strum.

To practice using your pick, try flicking forward to the **'Reading Guitar Tablature'** chapter.

Lesson 4: More Common Chord Changes

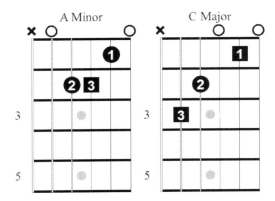

Take a look at the above two chord diagrams. The only difference between the chords of A minor[1] and C Major is that you move your 3rd finger onto the 5th string, 3rd fret.

Once you have mastered moving your 3rd finger from the A minor to the C Major, try taking your hand off the neck and placing C Major down on the neck from scratch. As we did before, place and remove the chord 10 times before starting to strum the C Major as you play it.

Don't worry about any buzzes as it is common to get a few rattles and muted notes in this chord at first. The easiest solution is to try to move your fingers closer to the fret wire and make sure you're right on the tips of your fingers.

When you're comfortable with that, play through the following **Audio Example 4a:**

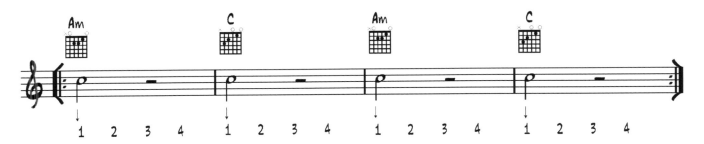

You may find this example is slightly easier than the one in the previous chapter, as this time we are only moving one finger.

Keep repeating these changes until you feel confident. If you like, you can increase the metronome speed slightly.

---

[1] In music, the convention is to use a capital 'M' for Major and a small 'm' for minor.

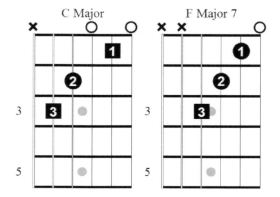

Once again, compare the above chords of C Major and F Major 7th. This time, only the 1st finger stays constant while you slide the 2nd and 3rd fingers down a string. Learn F Major 7th in the same was as you did before; first by moving there from C Major, and then by repetitively fingering the chord. When you're ready, practice the following example:

Audio Example 4b:

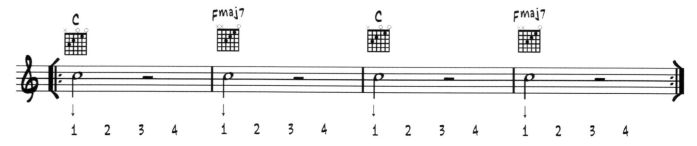

Notice that F Major 7th is only played on 4 strings.

Finally, we can combine all 4 chords from the previous chapters like this: **Audio Example 4c:**

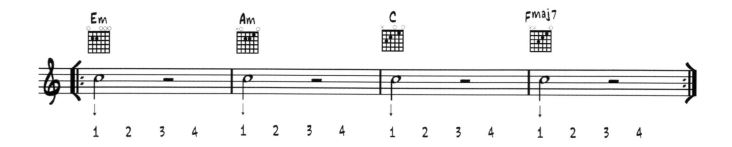

Feel free to experiment with some other chord combinations. Some good ones to begin with are as follows:

Audio Example 4d:

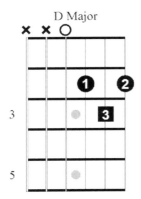

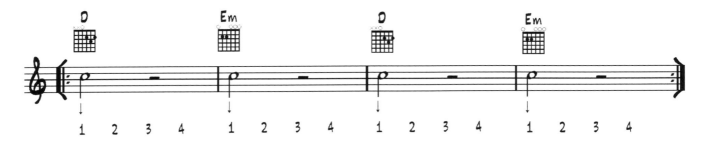

Audio Example 4e:

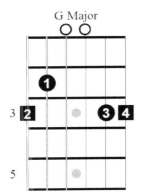

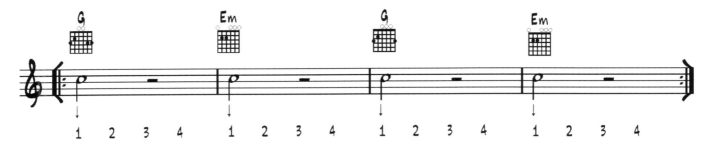

Audio Example 4f:

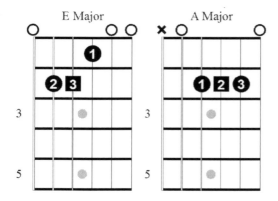

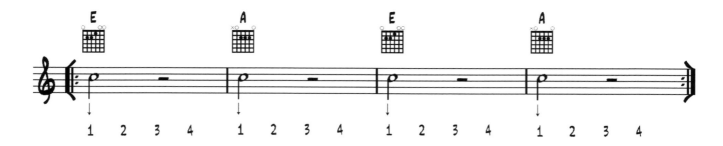

These are enough chords for now, but try mixing them up and playing them in new combinations. In the next chapter we'll look at how to add interest with rhythmic strumming patterns.

Lesson 5: Strumming

I make clear to all my private students that I am not a 'theory first' teacher. I prefer to get hands-on and have them making music as soon as possible. The one exception to this is in the way I teach rhythm and strumming.

Your strumming hand (normally your right if you're right-handed) only has two useful directions to hit the strings, *up* and *down*. If you understand why certain strums are *ups* and others are *downs* then it builds a fundamental security with rhythm. In fact, if you practice the following method, quite soon you'll never wonder how to play a rhythm again.

When we talk about rhythm in music, what we're essentially doing is breaking down a song into little chunks. That song might be a 3 minute Beatles tune or a 17 minute Rachmaninov symphony. Either way, we always arrange the rhythm the same way.

You may have heard the words *bars* and *beats* before. A beat is one pulse of a song: the distance from one click to the next on your metronome. Think of the beat as a one-syllable word. One beat of a piece of music looks like this:

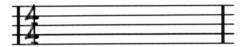

This note is called a **'Quarter Note'** as you can fit four of them in a bar, i.e., 4 ¼ notes = 1 bar.

A bar is a *container* for the beats, and at this stage **we will always have 4 beats in each bar.** An empty bar of music looks like this:

The 4/4 at the start tells us that there are 4 beats in the bar.

If we fill the bar with quarter notes it looks like this:

This is a whole load of preamble to get to one very simple rule:

Every time you see a ♩, you play a down strum.

Down strums are always on the beat, so if you're counting 1, 2, 3, 4 as in previous chapters, every time you say a number you strum downwards on the guitar.

Look at and listen to **Audio Example 5a:**

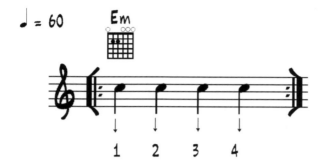

Set your metronome to play at 60 beats per minute, then play a down strum on each click while holding down the chord of E minor.

Try the same idea with A minor:

Audio Example 5b:

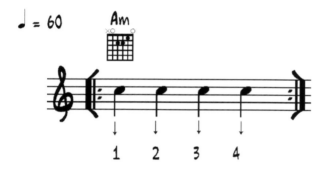

While this is a great method for developing good solid rhythm, music would be extremely dull if all our rhythms were like this.

One way to add interest is to double up on each quarter (1/4) note. In other words, imagine splitting each 1/4 note in half. This gives us 8 notes in the bar, and these are imaginatively called *1/8* or *eighth* notes.

On its own, an 1/8th note looks like this:

But when we put two of them next to each other, we join up their tails:

In other words, in music, instead of seeing two 1/8th notes written like this:

  , you would always see them written as .

You should, hopefully, see that two 1/8th notes take the same amount of time to play as one 1/4 note. So

takes the same amount of time to play as,

That is the end of the mathematics; I promise!

As you can see in the previous example, when we're playing 1/8th notes, our down strum is still in exactly the same place. All we need to do is squeeze in an up strum between each down. This up-strum should be exactly in the middle of each down.

On paper it looks like this:

Audio Example 5c:

Set your metronome to 60 beats per minute and begin by playing just a down strum on each click. When you're ready, add up strums in the middle of each down. Count out loud '1 and 2 and 3 and 4 and ', etc.

Listen to the Audio Example to help you.

Try the same idea with other chords like in **Audio Example 5d:**

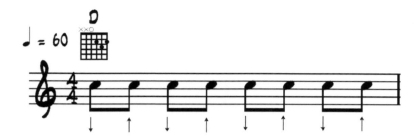

Once again, while we have added interest to our playing by adding more notes, music would be very repetitive if this was all the rhythm we ever played. Now let's learn to combine 1/4 notes and 1/8th notes to add variety.

Look at the following **Audio Example 5e:**

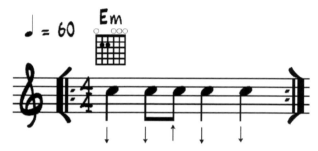

Beat 1 is a down strum, **beat 2** is a down and an up, **beat 3** is a down, as is **beat 4.**

Before you play, put the metronome on 60 and say out loud (no one needs to hear you!):

One. Two And Three. Four. – Down. Down-Up Down. Down.

Say it in time, rhythmically and confidently. Saying the rhythm out loud really helps your brain to process what it needs to do when it comes to strumming the rhythm in time.

When you're ready, strum it confidently. Don't worry about any buzzes in your fretting hand. Ignore them; we're only focusing on strumming.

When you're happy with the above, try **Audio Example 5f:**

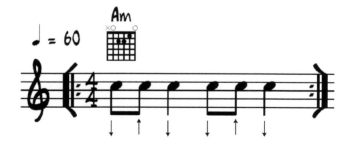

Say out loud *"One and Two. Three and Four. Down Up Down. Down Up Down."*

If it helps, you might want to think *jin gle bells jin gle bells.*

Throughout any rhythm you play on the guitar, the strumming hand never stops moving. It is constantly moving up and down in time. Downward movements are on the beats, upward movements are between the beats. This keeps you in time like a little built-in conductor. To create rhythms all we do is sometimes hit the strings and sometimes miss them.

Here are some other rhythms to practice:

Audio Example 5g:

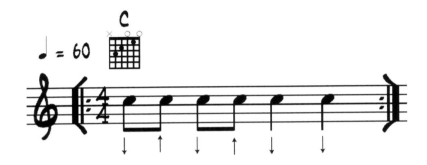

Down Up Down Up Down. Down.

Audio Example 5h:

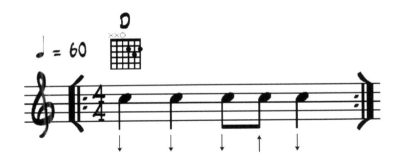

Down. Down. Down Up Down.

With each rhythm, remember to keep your strumming hand moving down and up all the time. To play a 1/4 note, simply don't strike the guitar on the up-strum.

Lesson 6: Changing Chords While Strumming

Now we have examined changing chords and strumming, let's bring the two ideas together. To help, I'm going to introduce a new musical sign. It is a 1/4 note rest. It looks like this:

𝄾

It simply means 'don't play for one beat.'

Study and listen to the following, (**Audio Example 6a**):

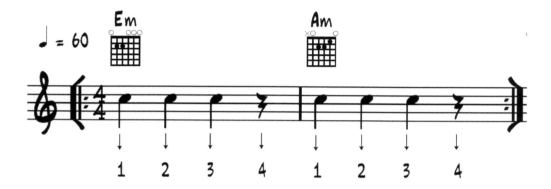

The strumming pattern is easy: **Down. Down. Down Rest**. On the rest, keep the right hand moving but just miss the strings. Don't forget to bring it back up ready for the **Down** of the second bar.

The rest on **beat 4** is very deliberate. It gives you extra time to change chord from E minor to A minor.

Begin with your metronome set on about 60 beats per minute. Feel free to slow it down if you can't quite manage the chord change yet. Start with three steady down strums on the E minor chord, and on **beat 4** slide your fingers across the strings adding your 1st finger to form A minor as you have previously practiced. Play the three down strums on A minor and then slide back to E minor. Keep repeating this sequence.

At this stage, DO NOT WORRY ABOUT BUZZING OR MUTED NOTES! In fact, don't worry about the quality of the sound. All we're learning is the muscle movement to get to A minor in time.

Imagine you're in a band playing in front of 50,000 people. Which do you think they'll notice more: the odd buzzy note or you completely stopping in the middle of a song?!

Keep playing, ignore any mistakes and keep focused on hitting the new chord on beat 1.

When you think you're doing ok with that, try this rhythmic idea in **Audio Example 6b:**

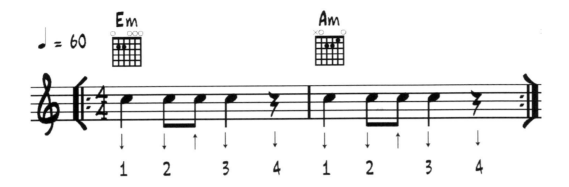

Always play with a metronome, ignore any fretting hand errors and make sure you hit beat 1 with the new chord on a down stroke.

Here's a slightly more complex rhythm:

Audio Example 6c:

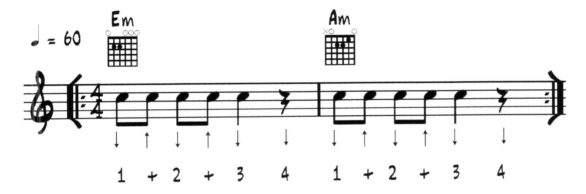

Apply the previous three rhythms to the following **2 bar** chord progressions:

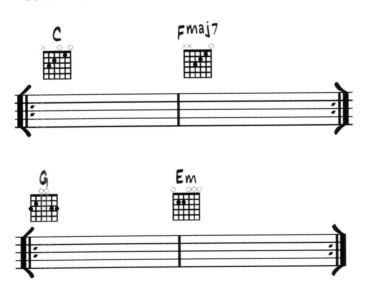

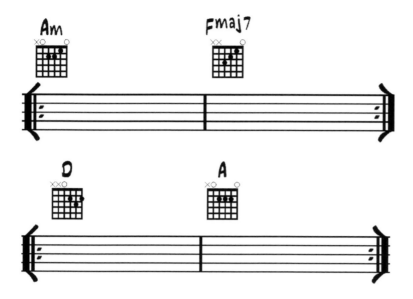

As you get better at this, try adding a down strum on **beat 4.** Here are some rhythms you might like to experiment with:

Try these rhythms with the previous chord progressions and, if you feel like it, dive into the chord dictionary at the back of the book and start experimenting with your own ideas.

Take a second to think about an acoustic song you know. When you break it right down, most songs are only a melody, chord progression and rhythm. It's a very cold way of looking at music and ignores a lot of other factors, but with just these three components you can play any song you like.

Lesson 7: New Chord Progressions to Practice

Here are some longer, 4 bar chord progressions you can practice. Start with just one strum per bar and then try varying the rhythm using ideas from the previous chapter:

1) **Audio Example 7a:**

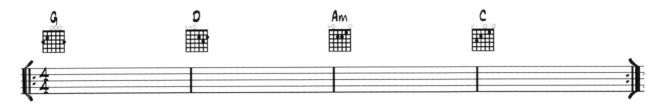

2) **Audio Example 7b:**

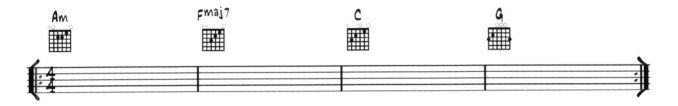

3) **Audio Example 7c:**

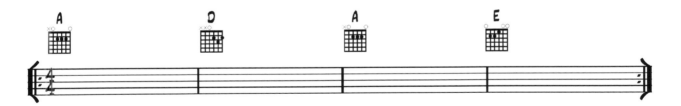

4) **Audio Example 7d:**

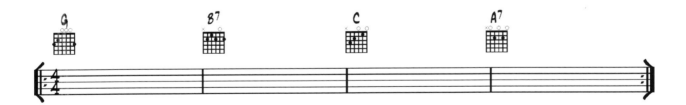

The B7 and A7 in the final progression are played like this:

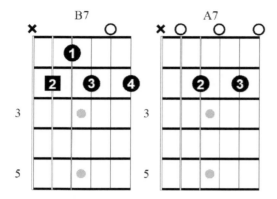

Remember, set your metronome on 60 to start with, and if it's too difficult to change chords in time, slow it down.

Also, there is no need to play right up to beat 4. Try using a rest on the final beat to give you time to move your fingers if you need to. Rhythm is still more important than tone at this stage.

Lesson 8: More Interesting Rhythms

The simplest and most common way of adding energy to your rhythm playing is to miss out strumming some down beats. To teach you this idea, we need to introduce a new musical symbol. It is an 1/8th note rest and looks like this:

Just like the 1/4 note rest from before, it simply means 'silence' or 'don't strum.' It will always be seen in combination with a strummed quarter note so that together they add up to **1 beat,** like this:

Before when we played the rhythm ♪♪ the strumming pattern was **Down Up.** So with the rhythm ⅞♪ , we are missing out the first **down** but we are still going to play the up stroke.

To make this easier, however, all guitarists move the strumming hand as if they are going to *play* the down strum, but we actually ***miss the strings.*** This keeps us in time.

In other words, our strumming hand is going up and down all the time, and we just *don't make contact* with the strings on the down strum.

To practice this idea, study the following **Audio Example 8a:**

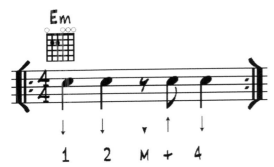

Count out loud: Down. Down. Miss Up Down.   Down. Down. Miss Up Down.

The 'M' in the above example stands for 'Miss'.

Now try holding down an E minor chord while you strum this rhythm. Remembering to keep the strumming hand moving all the time, miss the strings on **beat 3** and make contact on 'up' of **beat '3 and'.**

This is trickier but worth the effort.

Once you have this idea under your fingers, try this rhythm:

Audio Example 8b:

Down. Down Up Miss Up Down.

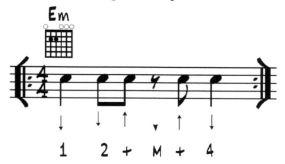

Finally, strum this:

Audio Example 8c:

Down. Miss Up Miss Up Down.

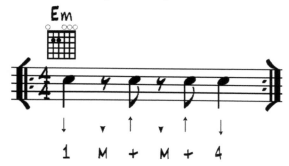

When you're comfortable with the idea of missing a down strum, transfer these rhythms to some of the easier chord changes we have looked at before. There is no need to make our tasks difficult for both hands at the same time. Try **Audio Example 8d** at 60 beats per minute:

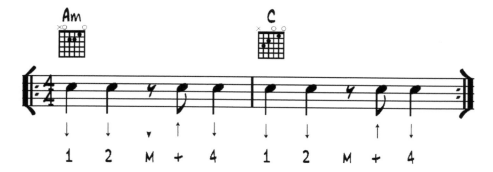

Here's one more example to spur your imagination. Spend as much time as you can mixing and matching chord changes and rhythms.

Audio Example 8e:

Down Up Miss Up Miss Up Down.

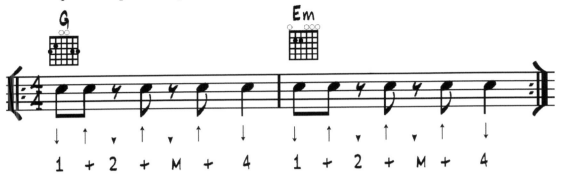

Now try making up your own rhythms.

Lesson 9: Splitting the Chord

An excellent way to give rhythmic and tonal variety to our strumming is to 'split' the strum into two separate string groups, the bass area and the chord area. By doing this we break up the chord and add an important extra dynamic into our music.

The most important thing to concentrate on is the correct bass note to target. For example, on an A minor chord the correct bass string is the 5th string, as it is on a C Major:

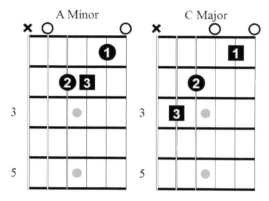

However on an E or G chord the bass note to play is on the 6th string:

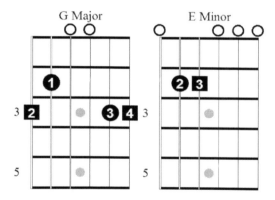

On a D or F chord you should play from the 4th string:

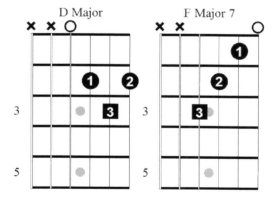

Until now we have just been using rhythmic notation to indicate when to strum. To communicate the split strum, I will show a chord like this in **Audio Example 9a:**

This isn't technically the *correct* notation, but it conveys the idea that you hit the bass note first and then the rest of the chord. In the above example you would hit the bass of the E minor chord on **beat 1** and the rest of the chord on **beat 2.**

You can also *double up* the strums like in **Audio Example 9b:**

The **down** strums are still hitting just the bass note, but now every **up** strum is hitting the rest of the chords.

When reading chord diagrams, pay attention to playing the correct bass notes. That said, however, it doesn't usually matter whether you hit just the bass note, or maybe the lowest 2 notes in the chord. In other words, don't be too tight in your strumming hand and don't be too precise.

Here are a few examples to get you going.

Audio Example 9c:

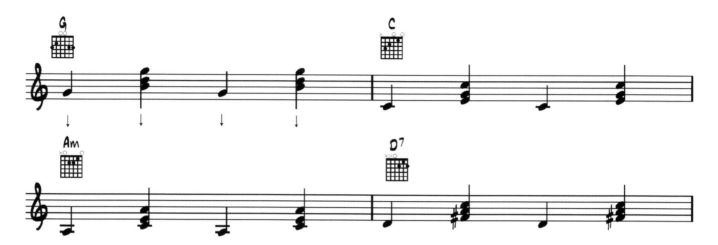

Audio Example 9d:

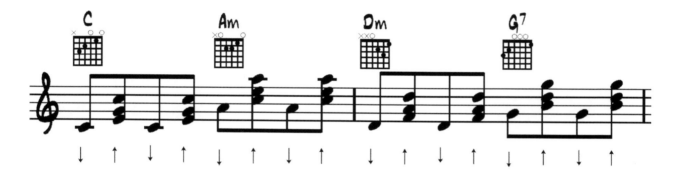

New chords:

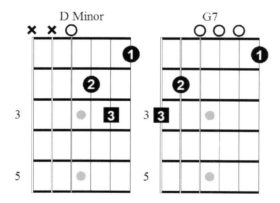

Notice that between D minor and G7 the 1st finger doesn't move.

Lesson 10: Descending Bass Lines

Descending bass lines are an extremely common idea that help us to link certain chords together. Look at the following three chords:

Audio Example 10a:

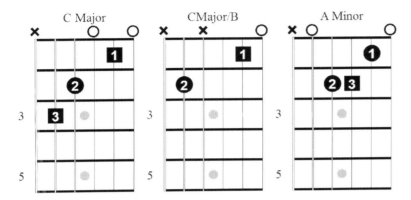

You already know C Major and A minor; however the chord in the middle is new. If you study the second chord, you will see that the notes on the 1st, 2nd and 3rd strings are identical to the C Major chord.

The main difference between the first two chords is that the bass note on the 5th string has *descended* by one fret, i.e, it has moved from the 3rd fret down to the 2nd. This downward bass movement *resolves* nicely to the open 5th string in A minor.

Try playing through the above chords in order, but instead of strumming straight through each chord, split each one; pick the 5th string first and then strum the rest of the chord.

On the C Major / B chord try to avoid playing the 4th string.

Audio Example 10b:

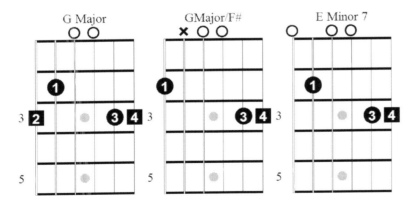

The same concept is happening in the above chord progression. Focus on bringing out the bass line on the 6th string.

These ideas happen all the time in many pop songs, from The Beatles to Fleetwood Mac. Check out this example, which is similar to a famous 'Mac song:

Audio Example 10c:

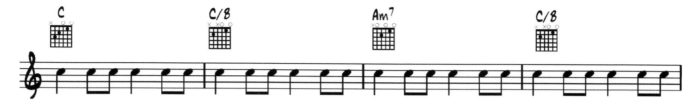

Again, try splitting the 5th string from the rest of the chord in your strumming to highlight the bass line.

Here's an idea that has been used by many British 'indie' groups:

Audio Example 10d:

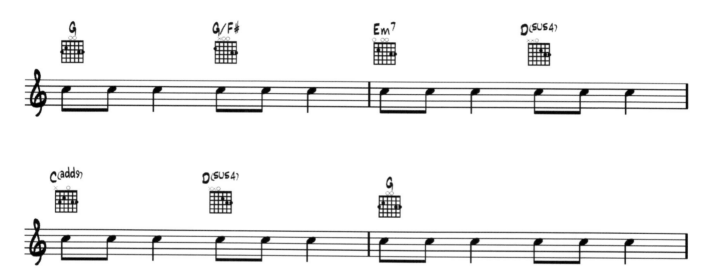

Focus on bringing out the bass line.

The chords you might not know from the previous example are the following:

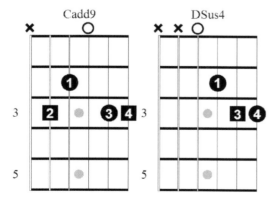

Finally, here is another common motif:

Audio Example 10e:

Lesson 11: Fragments of Songs

For copyright reasons, I can't give you full songs here, but for study purposes have a look at this chord progression and rhythm in the style of Green Day.

Audio Example 11a:

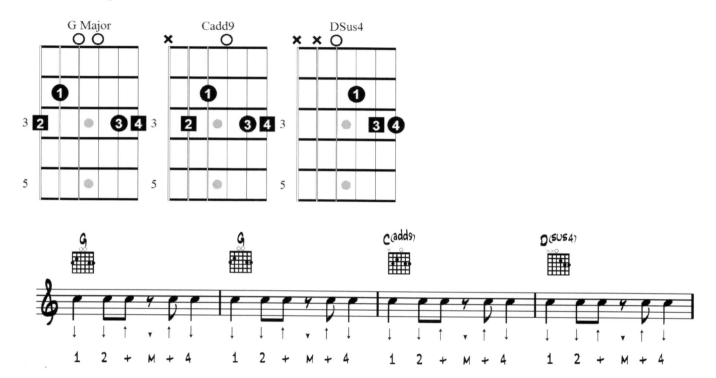

Here is another tune in the style of Eagle Eye Cherry:

Audio Example 11b:

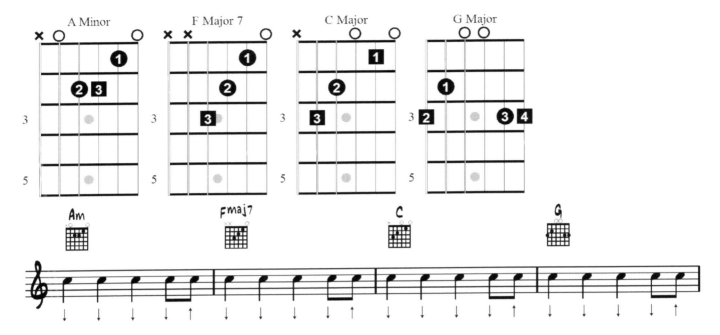

In the previous example, try playing the first two down strums just on the bass notes of the chord, then the remaining '**down down up**' on the top few strings.

This idea is in the style of Oasis:

Audio Example 11c:

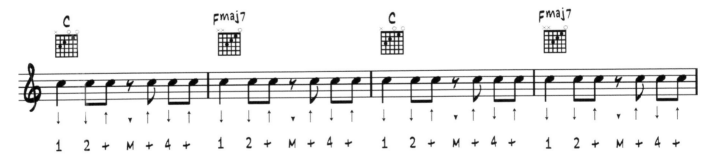

Try to make it sound bouncy.

Here's one in the style of Simon and Garfunkel:

Audio Example 11d:

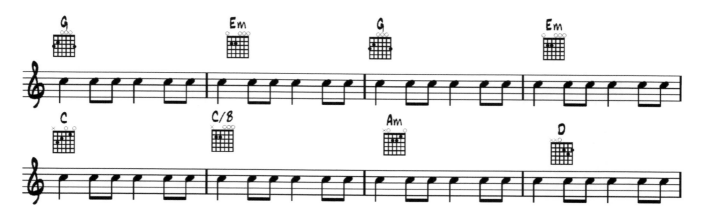

Lesson 12: Reading Guitar Tablature

Guitar tablature is an extremely efficient way of communicating music on the guitar. It's been around for over 400 years and dates back to the Baroque period when Bach used it to write out his Lute Suites.

It is easy to read, and unlike standard music notation it does not involve learning a new language.

Guitar tablature has six lines, one for each guitar string. We simply write the number of the fret which we wish to play on the appropriate line/string.

Look at this:

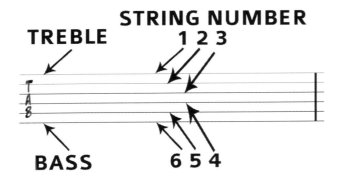

The word TAB is normally written at the start of each line to remind us what we're reading. It has a hidden benefit that the 'B' is at the bottom to help us remember that the lowest line is the **bass** string on the guitar. The 'T' at the top could stand for **treble.** In the diagram above, I have numbered each line to correspond with each guitar string. The bass or 6th string is at the bottom and the highest, thinnest string, (1), is at the top.

It is now simply a case of writing a fret number on each line to tell you which notes to play.

Study the tablature line of the following example.

Audio Example 12a:

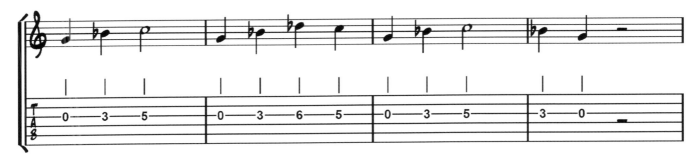

All the notes are played on the 3rd string. The '0' indicates that the 3rd string should be picked with no fretted note. The 3 means 'play the 3rd fret on the 3rd string' and the '5' means 'play the 3rd string with the 5th fret held down.'

If you play through the previous example, you should begin to hear a famous tune by a band called Deep Purple.

Here are a few other simple melodies to get you going. Remember to hold your pick properly and be careful of your posture. Don't forget to only read the lower line with the numbers; you can ignore all the dots.

Audio Example 12b:

Star Wars.

Audio Example 12c:

London's Burning:

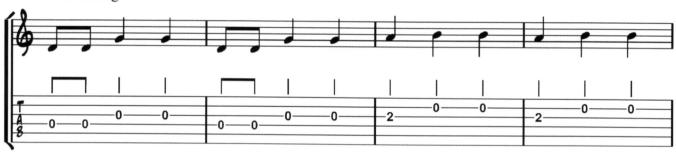

Audio Example 12d:

The Simpsons:

Lesson 13: Finger Picking Patterns

The most common and effective way to decorate your chords and add melodic interest to your playing is to use finger picking patterns with your right hand. Instead of strumming each chord with a pick, you will use your thumb and fingers to pick one string at a time.

I will give you some easy and useful patterns to get you started. Before you panic at the piece of tablature below, note that all the numbers, (fretted notes) **are already held down as part of your chord.** In other words, as soon as you have your chord held down, you do not need to move your fretting hand.

Look at the following:

Audio Example 13a:

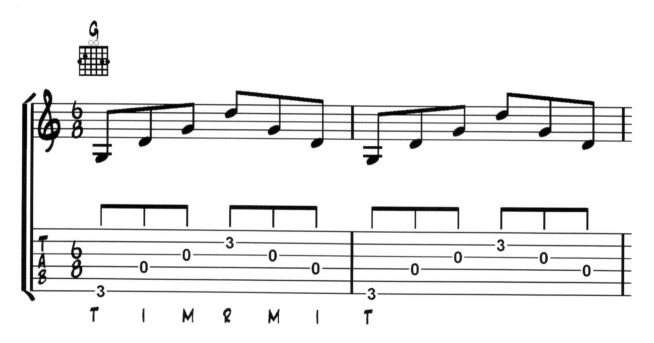

As in the previous chapter, ignore the dots and focus on the tablature. Hold down the chord of G Major and look at it.

Your 2nd finger is playing the 3rd fret on the 6th string.
Your 1st finger is playing the 2nd fret on the 5th string.
Your 3rd finger is playing the 3rd fret on the 2nd string.
Your 4th finger is playing the 3rd fret on the 1st string.

Can you see how these notes are reflected in the tablature? As we pick through the strings, hopefully you can see that we do not need to move our fretting hand at all.

The letters under the notes stand for:

Thumb, **I**ndex finger, **M**iddle finger, **R**ing finger.
We will use these exact fingers to play through the previous example.

When you are comfortable with this idea, try changing chords in time as in **Audio Example 13b:**

Always be aware of what your bass note is. Your thumb should always pick the bass note in this style.

Try to keep your picking hand flat; there should be no arch in it.

The thumb should be closer to the neck of the guitar than the fingers and should always push down across the bass string.

The picking fingers should curl into the hand when you pick each note. Never pick so your hand moves away from the guitar.

Finally, always *start* with your fingers touching the first strings they will play. Make the strings sound by pulling your fingers away from the string.

Here are some other common finger picking patterns for you to try:

Play example 13c evenly; count **1 & 2 & 3 & 4 &.**

Audio Example 13c:

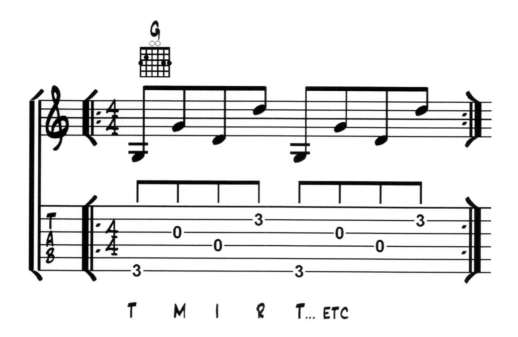

T   M   I   R   T... ETC

When you're confident, try changing to a new chord.

Audio Example 13d is similar to the previous one, but the thumb takes care of two bass notes, not just one:

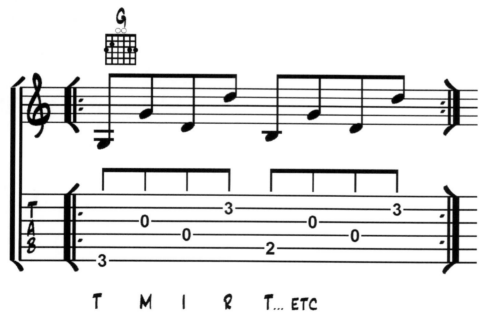

T   M   I   R   T... ETC

Again, try extending this to some of your favourite chord changes. Keeping in rhythm is key.

Audio Example 13e involves playing two notes at the same time, one with the thumb, one with the ring finger:

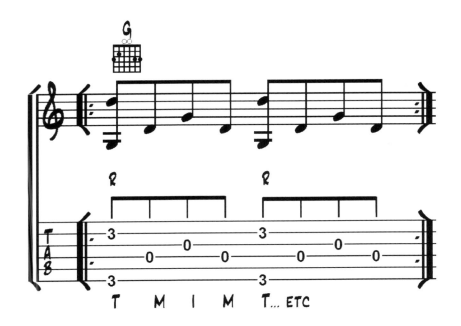

Audio Example 13f is a sequence you can practice to learn to change chords smoothly:

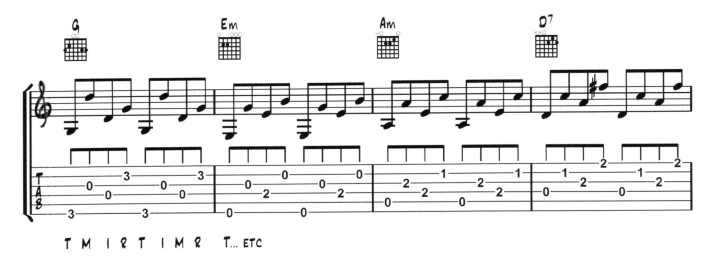

One final comment, just because I have written a pattern on a specific set of strings doesn't mean you have to play it there. Try experimenting with other string groups.

As always, go slow and play it correctly before you speed up the metronome.

Have fun!

Joseph

Lesson 14: Dictionary of Useful Chords

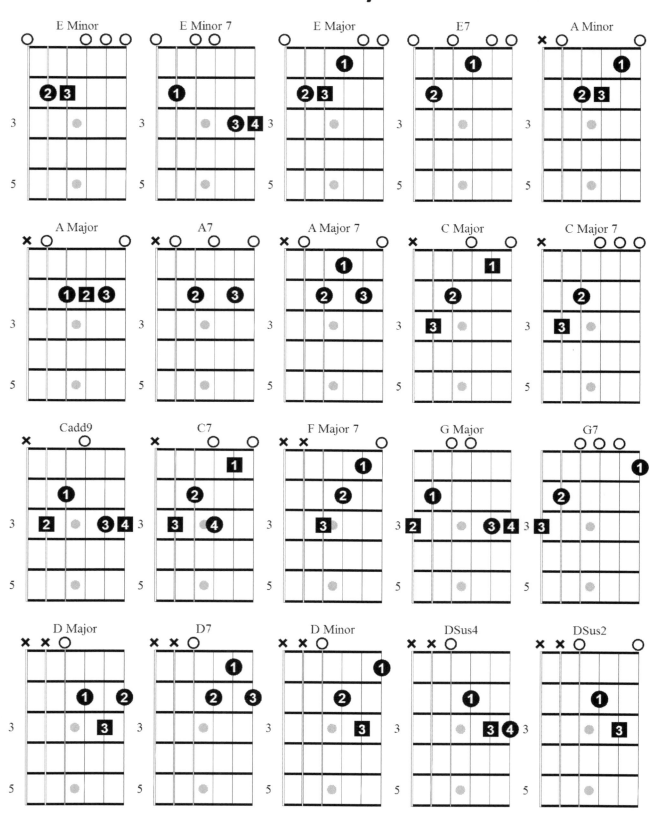

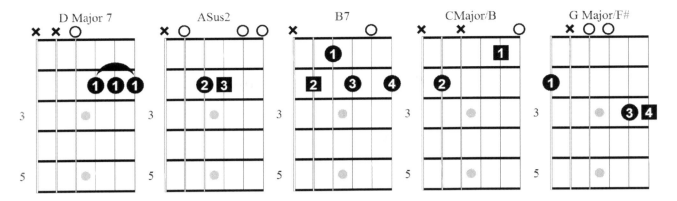

There are, of course many other chords; however, my advice would to be focus on these ones first. They're the most common chords you will come across as a beginner.

Lesson 15: Further Study

As I mentioned in the introduction, I don't think Skype lessons are particularly beneficial for beginners, however, if you have come this far, please feel free to contact me via **www.fundamental-changes.com** if you would like to continue your education through Skype lessons.

The website contains over 200 free guitar lessons and is growing daily.

YouTube is an incredible resource for the guitar. If you want to learn a song, just search for "<song name> Guitar Lesson" and you will usually find it.

The Registry of Guitar Teachers has produced some great graded books for acoustic guitar. After working through this book, I would recommend their **grade 2 book**.

If you're more interested in rock and blues guitar, I recommend the series of **graded books** by Rock School.

If you like blues guitar, you can check out my **Complete Guide to Blues Guitar Books** as these provide good material to progress the beginner guitarist.

I have written eighteen books all about different aspects of playing the guitar. You can find a list on the following page.

Have fun,

Joseph

Other Books by the Author

Fundamental Changes in Jazz Guitar I: The Major ii V I for Bebop Guitar

Minor ii V Mastery for Jazz Guitar

Jazz Blues Soloing for Guitar

Guitar Scales in Context

Guitar Chords in Context: Part One

Drop 2 Chord Voicings for Jazz and Modern Guitar

The CAGED System and 100 Licks for Blues Guitar

The Complete Guide to Playing Blues Guitar Book One: Rhythm Guitar

The Complete Guide to Playing Blues Guitar Book Two: Melodic Phrasing

The Complete Guide to Playing Blues Guitar Book Three: Beyond Pentatonics

The Complete Guide to Playing Blues Guitar: Compilation

The Complete Technique, Theory and Scales Compilation for Guitar

Sight Reading Mastery for Guitar

Complete Technique for Modern Guitar

Rock Guitar Un-CAGED: The CAGED System and 100 Licks for Rock Guitar

Be Social

Join over 4000 people getting six free guitar lessons each day on Facebook:

www.facebook.com/FundamentalChangesInGuitar

Keep up to date on Twitter

@Guitar_Joseph

Printed in Great Britain
by Amazon